Little Bastards of Yorkville

ARTHUR MILLER

outskirts
press

Table of Contents

Prologue

Old Yorkville, one of New York City's most interesting and diverse neighborhoods, was a place that, like many of the City's old neighborhoods, will never come back, at least not in the same way. The Yorkville of the early 1950s was an area that yielded many intense memories, good and bad, pleasurable and sad. Memories populated by people who are no longer with us but who gave the neighborhood its character.

My intention in writing this book is to bring the flavor of the people, the streets, and the events to you the reader, and make them live for you through the eyes of those who remember them well.

I hope you will find this book humorous as well as informative as the events described could only have been perpetrated, and I do use the word appropriately, by the characters who came out of this time and place. Four characters will take you through an unusual tour of old Yorkville. Enjoy the ride.

Introduction

The Yorkville of the 1950's was a neighborhood of old tenements sprinkled with a few high risers that were the harbingers of what would happen to that most interesting part of the city. The area, which stretched from East 79th Street to 96th Street and from the East River to 3rd Avenue in Manhattan, has since become one of the most expensive chunks of real estate in New York City. This, of course, was not always the case. Walk up tenements have mostly been replaced by high-rise buildings replete with doormen and concierges. Shi- shi restaurants sport their awnings where dark neighborhood saloons, pungent delicatessens and miniscule candy stores once stood. Young yuppies with their lattes and boutique canines have since replaced the blue-collar working class families of yore. Walking down any block one could catch snippets of German, Gaelic, Czech, Hungarian, Italian, a smattering of Spanish conversations, a veritable tower of Babel.

We lived in the heart of Yorkville, my friends and I, with parents who struggled to put bread on the table, living the lives of hard work and dreams shared by many of the early immigrants. We were poor and, while knowing it full well, we didn't know. This apparent contradiction was made true perhaps because everyone was in the "same boat".

Carl Schurtz Park, flanking the East River Drive was our backyard. Then, only the rich and famous inhabited the imposing high risers that lined York Avenue from 79th Street all the way to uptown 90th Street. Gracie Mansion, the mayor's residence on 88th Street, was the crowning jewel in this string of luxury. Our elementary school, Public School 158 stood then as it does still, presenting its imposing gray stone façade to York Avenue. It ranks now, as it did then, as one of the top performing schools in the City but its true mark of distinction is to have had Jimmy Cagney as one of its pupils.

For us, the high-rise structures may just as well have been an area in the fourth dimension. They were there but inaccessible, and we thought of their occupants in the same light. Famous people from the early days of TV and movies like Don Ameche, Arthur Godfrey, Walter Cronkite, Basil Rathbone, Robert Alda were spotted on a regular basis.

When I was a boy of six, my mother would bring me to the promenade skirting Carl Schurtz Park that faces the East River. There I would fasten my key skates to my shoes and skate for hours. For anyone under the age of thirty let me explain that key skates consisted of the mandatory four wheels anchored to a metal platform with two clamps on either side. A key would be inserted in the metal base and the turning of the key would affix the clamps to the soles of the shoes. Great care had to be taken in executing this procedure or risk flying head first and making a sudden contact with the cemented ground as the offending skate disengaged itself from the sole of your shoe as you so innocently sped along brushing past startled casual strollers.

On an almost weekly basis a mob of screaming members of the fairer sex could be seen running by in hot pursuit (is there a cold pursuit?) of a man who appeared to be trying his best to escape this determined posse. My mother would later tell me the man was Lawrence Tierney, the star of the Dillinger movie. Since this scene repeated itself many times as Mr. Tierney was seen running on a regular basis, it leads one to believe that he must have been willing to risk life and limb to be showered with the adulation.

We had the local libraries, the movie houses that showed double features, newsreels and cartoons, affordable transportation and, yes, some restaurants and many German beer halls. We were in a poor man's Camelot and we didn't even know it.

CHAPTER 1

It Begins

"THAT'S MY HOPALONG Cassidy card!" The little boy screamed out angrily. The other boy, much larger and older by two years would not release the treasure to its rightful owner but rather waved the card over the boy's head in a taunting motion. "Take it from me!" Paul shouted while still waving it over the young boy's head. Artie went for the throat. A few blows, kicks, and other damages later, Artie held the now wrinkled prize in his shaking hand. A pyrrhic victory to be sure, it was the battle of his life for Artie. "Arthur!" his mother shouted as she rushed to the scene of the bloody skirmish. Quite shaken by the sight of her battle scarred little boy, she tried to pull him away. As if by magic, out of nowhere, a crowd of kids had gathered to the site of the brief skirmish hoping to see more serious damage and chafing to know why it had started.

Fights were among the favorite forms of entertainment for the older kids and teens on the block. But in addition, when no fights were brewing, the neighborhood boys would fill their days with games of stickball, stoopball while the girls played potsy or jump rope. At times the two would get together to play a game of ring- a- levio.

Stickball, the city's street version of baseball, was played throughout the five boroughs of the City. Home plate was usually a manhole cover in the street with parked cars designated as the bases. A pink rubber ball made by the Spalding Company, hence the name "Spalding ball" was pitched to a hitter on a bounce. The bat was usually a stick salvaged from a discarded broom or mop. The game was played by the older boys and the "little guys" were only allowed to watch and not get in the way. Sometimes they would retrieve a lost ball or be sent to buy a soda at the local candy store. This was reward enough for being allowed to hang near the older guys.

Stoopball was the game of the younger kids. The same pink, Spalding rubber ball would be struck against a stoop, hence the name of the game. The stoop, a favorite gathering place for young and old alike, was a few stone steps which led to the entrance of the tenements. The idea was to hit the sharp edge of the stoop with the ball and then run the bases which were fashioned from pieces of cardboard or drawn on the pavement with a piece of chalk.

Game of Stoopball

Public domain photo from the Internet

The rules of stoopball were much like Major League Baseball's except there was no pitcher or catcher. The ball, once struck against the edge of the said stoop would fly out to the anxious fielders of boys who eagerly awaited to catch it and score an out. Quite often the game would be interrupted by pedestrians trying to cross the street and occasionally by an irate taxi driver who, after blaring his horn in an unsuccessful attempt to make the kids move , would lean out of the driver's window and shout: "Get out of the way you little bastard!"

The teams were chosen by one or two of the bigger boys, as the rest of us, in a pecking order, would plead to be chosen to play on the same side with one of the "captains" who was most always older and stronger than we were. Being one of the youngest boys, I found myself, most often than not, left out of the games. My only hope was to be an errand boy, which entailed trips to one of the local delis with orders to return with sandwiches, sodas and various sweets. On these occasions I would exact my revenge for not being chosen by biting off the ends of a hero sandwich they ordered me to buy with the skill of a surgeon or, even syphon off about an inch from the top of their sodas. This latter maneuver took some skill as the tops of the bottles were securely protected with metal caps. Once opened, they had to be replaced very carefully so that its owner would not suspect it had been tampered with. I never backwashed.

Teams changed faster than Hollywood marriages and games lasted until an unresolvable altercation occurred, which happened more often than not. The rules of the game were simple. The "hitter" would attempt to strike a sharp corner of one of the steps with the ball. Once contact was made, the "hitter" would run the bases with the object of reaching home plate. Since we played from the sidewalk to the street, anything and anyone could interrupt the games, not only pedestrians or irate taxi drivers but angry janitors who wanted to sweep the area and, at times, the no nonsense neighborhood foot patrolman. Fair and foul lines were drawn with chalk and the ball field boundaries were either parked cars, street signs or even an occasional garbage pail. Many a game was ruined when home plate, a designated parked car, decided to coast down the street piloted by its clueless driver. We became very adept at dodging janitors wielding brooms or housewives flinging pots of water from tenement windows in an attempt to make us disperse whenever the noise level reached the red zone in the decibel scale.

Girls would have their own games and very rarely would the sexes join ranks and engage in one of these street games. Rope jumping and Potsy were the most popular on the street as they were the easiest to learn and cost just pennies.

Game of Potsy
Public domain photo
from the Internet

The game of Potsy was made up of painted or chalked boxes on the ground with different numbers in each box. A player would flip a bottle cap to land on one of the boxes. With the dexterity of a tightrope walker, the player would jump on one foot to the square containing the cap and, while still balancing on one foot, would bend down and retrieve the bottle cap and flip it into another box next in line. Each box had a value according to the number on it. If the bottle cap rolled out of the numbered boxes or did not follow the number pattern, the player was out of the game. Sometimes, the line of girls waiting to enter the game was as long as the "Rockettes" chorus line.

Johnny on a Pony was a much rougher game played by boys. One boy would place his back against a wall. Right behind him would be a line of boys bent over like horses and pressed tightly, head to back to form a human bridge. A team, usually equal in number to the bent over group, would one by one jump on the backs of these and jockey into position at the front of the line. If the jumping group could cause the defenders to collapse,

 victory was theirs. If not, the pony boys would win and the positions would be changed.

Johnny on a Pony

Public domain picture from the Internet

Ring- a- levio was played by both sexes. A makeshift "prison" was formed from a cellar space down a flight of stairs or in some corner that lay between two buildings. One team would hide within an agreed area (usually the outer boundary was around the street corner) and the other team had to find them. One by one, members of the hiding team were cap- tured and brought to the "prison". One of the uncaptured had to free those in jail by touching the captures and shouting: "ring- a- levio, one, two, three." The game was over when all of the opposing team was captured. The game could last for hours until someone's mother shouted: ""Dinner!"

The streets were our play ground and there we would play our games all day long without even having a dime in our pocket. Tired and sweaty we would break only for lunch or dinner or, on weekdays, for homework

"Bubble gum", as the name suggests, was a stick of gum (3inches wide and 3 inches long) that could be blown up by a chewer to a large bubble that, at times, would blow up all over the chewer's face. The bubble gum came in pack- ets along with trading cards such as Hopalong Cassidy (for which I risked life and limb), super heroes, science fiction, adventure, history and so on. For anywhere from a penny to a nickel, we could go to a neighborhood deli or candy store and plunk down our coins for a pack of gum and cards. The gum was usually tossed away in favor of the collectable cards that lay in wait inside the covered package.

The goal for every one of was to have a complete set of a particular series of cards. One way or another, I would satisfy this goal either by purchase or by contest or by "flipping" for it. These cards had a front side with a picture and a backside with related writing on it. One "dope" was the designated first flipper. He would throw a card which landed either front or back side up called heads or tails respectively. The other kids in the contest had to flip one of their cards and if "heads" matched "heads" and "tails" matched "tails" the cards would be theirs. If there was no match, the "dope" won. The "dope" seldom won as cheating was rampant, more so if a card were really desirable. This swindling occurred through a fast switching of cards, intimidation or, a host of other tricks.

Comic books, which were sold exclusively in candy stores, were another item of common interest. They were usually at the rear of the establishment where, in addition to browsing in the comic section, we would sneak a look at the spicy magazines of the day. I can remember purchasing the first issue of Mad Magazine for ten cents. Had I kept the issue I would be a rich man today.

The two rival emporiums of sweets, Bursky's and Winkler's, where we would plunk our pennies, were located on 79th Street and York Avenue. Bursky's

was not so popular as the proprietor did not allow us to hang out. Bursky's, the former, was not as fussy. His linoleum floor never met a broom or a mop. Flies never landed on the glass counter top which had the sticky sheen of flypaper and the dirty rags on display behind the counter were a testament to his attempt at cleaning. It was said that old man Bursky could be seen, after hours, rinsing out the used cone shaped wax paper soda cups and replacing them on the rack ready for use the next day. Mr. Bursky would have never passed muster with the health code inspector but he certainly was ahead of his time as far as recycling.

As a boy, I used to hoard my comic book collection under the twin bed that took up most of the floor space in my very small bedroom. My Mother and I lived in this tiny, fifth floor walk up apartment on 81st street which today commands a hefty Manhattan rent.

Comic books were traded and gambled for with the same passion as the trading cards. Many a fistfight would break out over an uneven trade or a purloined comic. I wish I had kept the much-loved collection. But, in retrospect, it was thanks to the comics that I became a proficient early reader. Once a week, on Sunday mornings, the radio stations hosted programs for children with the weekly comic section on the newspapers. The Daily News, the Journal American and the Mirror were the big three journals that featured a slew of cartoon characters that in addition to Blondie, Dick Tracy and the Phantom, were Terry and the Pirates, Mandrake the Magician, Maggie & Jiggs, Smiling Jack and others.

I would spread open the "funnies" section of the newspaper on our living room/bedroom floor and eagerly wait for the man who would read the entire comic section with his young listeners to begin. Having no television, the radio and print media were the primary forms of entertainment. Being immersed in the world of comics and the "funnies" it was a natural evolution when I began to emulate the drawings with my own pencil and paper. I would spend hours drawing and became quite good at it, winning the praise of my second grade teacher who believed that art was in my future. For pennies, I could have some sketching paper and drawing pencils and became quite proficient in expressing several shades of gray in the renderings of Dick Tracy, Sam Ketchum, Archie and many more. I was in my gray period. Mrs. Balsam, my second grade teacher encouraged me to enter my drawings in a contest. I didn't win and was quite disappointed. By fifth grade I quit all drawing feeling that I was not good enough and would never be good enough since I could not draw my original cartoons. A part of my personality was emerging; a part that drove me to always be the best at something.

Cartoon characters drawn at age seven

As we went up the grades, the early street games were left behind in favor of the more sophisticated sports of baseball, football and basketball. All of us boys had a burning desire to excel in one or more of these games. I recall spraining all of my fingers by catching a baseball barehanded since I had no glove. Quitting was never an option. One day my mother surprised me with the gift of the oh so desired baseball glove. This she had acquired through the redemption of trading stamps. Supermarket shoppers would receive these stamps as a reward for shopping at their store. Carefully, each week, she would paste them into small booklets that, upon reaching a certain point value, could be redeemed for various items. The glove was a pitiful affair with no padding and no "pocket." When the blazing ball came my way, the fingers of the glove would flap back and the impact was just as painful but, I looked official, just like the other players.

Baseball was our summer sport; football and basketball were our winter games. My football gear was a layer of shirts under a shapeless, oversized jacket. After a time, the game became too painful and, in order to spare some bones, I switched to basketball.

Looking back now I can't quite pinpoint when it all started. Perhaps the many bumps and bruises received in the spirit of competitive sports contributed to the beginning of my troublemaking years. What I do know is that my career as a troublemaker started quite early. To my mother's chagrin, the teachers at PS 158 informed her that I was a "high strung " child and put me on half day in kindergarten.

At the ripe age of seven, I committed my first ignoble deed. Around the corner from our tenement building, on 81st Street and East End Avenue, stood a factory. One flight up from the main entrance was a heavy metal door which, when opened, led to a large open area where a group of overall clad factory workers labored over their tasks. With the creative brain of a seven year old I had excogitated the following deed: I would pick up an old newspaper from the trash bin, hunt around the sidewalks for dog poop, scoop it up in said newspaper, go up the one flight of stairs to the heavy metal door and knock with all of my might. The great metal door would swing open with a sonorous creak. At that point I would hurl the poop and paper in the interior, fly down the stairs and run like hell. This ritual, I confess, I repeated many times without being caught, a testament to the speed I had developed in playing all those street games.

CHAPTER **2**

The Good Folk Of Yorkville

IN THE NEIGHBORHOOD there were two grocery stores on the same side of 81st Street that competed for the business that was available to them. The locals, who had no checking accounts or readily available cash, avoided the A&P supermarket and did their shopping at Mr. Salinski's or Mr. Stern's deli. Salinski's was our favorite because he extended my mother credit which she tried to pay up week after week. On Mr. Salinski's counter, which rivaled Mr. Stern's in long ago spilled and forgotten condiments, rested a large glass jar of mustard. A flat wooden stick the length of a ruler only wider rested inside the mustard jar. He would, as many customers could attest, at times, drop the "spoon" on the floor that also rivaled Mr. Stern's in the degree of benign neglect. Wrapped around his mid section was an apron that, to anybody's guess, must have been white once upon a time but now sported many shades of unidentifiable colors. Once having retrieved the "spoon" he would carefully wipe it on said apron. Despite this flagrant disregard for basic cleanliness, I loved the hero sandwiches that he prepared. The shelves were lined with rows and rows of cans and boxes of all types of food. One could detect a fine layer of dust enveloping this display. God only knows what insect strain or bacterial anomaly inhabited the hidden spaces behind the soup cans and hero loaves.

"Hey kid," Mr. Salinski would call out from behind the counter, "Wanna make ten cents?" He would give the neighborhood kids ten cents to wash his car. Of course I would jump at the chance faster that a bum on a bologna sandwich. No sooner was the job done than I would plunk down the hard earned dime on the counter for a pack of gum and trading cards.

The favorite pastime for young and old alike, including children, was to hang out on the stoop. We all formed a loose social network. The latest gossip would be eagerly exchanged even though everyone already knew everyone else's business thanks to the conversations drifting up the narrow airshaft separating the tenement buildings.

Loretta , a middle age woman, was one of the regulars. On a warm day, her bare feet sported the most gargoyle like toenails. They were long and curved and reminiscent of a bird of prey, a bird whose long talons could wrap around tree limbs. The ugliness of the toenails was only surpassed by her heavily calloused feet. Needless to say, both were brown with encrusted dirt. Day in and day out Loretta wore the same loose fitting house -dress with a blackened collar, blackened from repeated exposure to her sweaty neck. But, it must be said, that Loretta was never seen without rollers in her hair, rollers that I now suspect, were never removed. As kids we would tease each other and taunt: "Would you do it? Would you do it?" referring of course to the sexual act.

On the other end of the spectrum was Regis, a part proprietor of the ritzy French restaurant "Le Boeuf a la Mode" which was located next door. Regis resembled a spinning top, all upper body perched on spindly legs. He always wore a black suit whose shine cried out for cleaning. Regis was a thorn in the side of his partner who, being French, looked down his nose on the motley crew hanging out on the stoop adjacent to his restaurant. Regis loved cats and, after hours, would collect all the strays from the neighborhood and bring them into the restaurant and gave them free reign of the bar and restaurant area. Fortunately for the cats, this was a French restaurant but Regis carried the scent of his furry friends wherever he went.

My mother, Teddy, the yenta in residence, Jeanette, the sister I never had and her mother were among the ranks of the less colorful stoop dwellers. Stella on the other hand, shone brightly in this constellation. Rumors of her sexual appetite were well known and it was said that gender and age mattered little in her preference. On one occasion, Stella dropped her dust mop from her open window and down the airshaft that connected two buildings. Bill, who lived in the adjacent building, very obligingly volunteered to retrieve the mop and deliver it to her second floor apartment. A few hours passed and Bill's absence was all but forgotten until Aggie, his wife, happened by and inquired about her husband's whereabouts, at which time she was informed that Bill was seen going up to Stella's apartment sporting the fallen dust mop . Oh yes, that was about two hours ago.

It was said that Aggie, an intelligent and frail woman who suffered from "nerves" had let the bottle get the better of her, however, upon receiving the news, she disappeared and shortly thereafter was seen running out of her ground floor apartment brandishing a huge cast iron frying pan with all the fervor of a Samurai warrior entering into battle. We, the stoop spectators, watched Aggie fly up the stairs to Stella's apartment and we knew exactly what would happen next. A few minutes of silence passed and then the calm was shattered. Shattered by piercing screams, screams that accompanied the sonorous whacks of cast iron as it made contact with Bill's bald head. Moments later, Bill was seen running out of the apartment with his hands over his bald head in a desperate but futile attempt to block the blows of the frying pan that were so deftly administered by Aggie. Aggie and Bill were followed out of the apartment and down the stairs by Stella who, in an advance state of undress, joined the uproar with her own fevered screeching and shouting. As this motley trio raced by us , panic engulfed Bill, furiously wielding Aggie and flailingly disrobed Stella we , the stoop dwellers, doubled over in good merriment. Aggie's salacious expletives rivaled what could be uttered by a drunken stevedore who just stubbed his big toe. Finally this motley parade came to a halt at the entrance of Bill's apartment where he, in a Houdini like fashion, managed to elude the rest of the blows,from the wildly swaying frying pan. I saw him the next day as he tried to dodge my hello. His bald head was covered with large bumps and he sported two black eyes. All for the cause of a fallen dust mop.

These burlesque like scenes were quite common on our block. Everyone knew who did what to whom and how and when thanks to the airshaft between the buildings.

Things did not stay quiet for long and Stella was back in center stage so as not to disappoint the front stoop constituency. I recall a hysterical but nearly tragic incident in which she was the star. The superintendent of the five buildings known as Odhall Court was a powerful man by the name of Mr. Grinjon. He was an excellent chess player whom I could never beat and we would play between the brawls that occurred on a regular basis between him and his wife or other protagonists, depending on the day. Mrs. Grijon was taller, heavier and probably stronger than her husband. Both were Russian and when sober, were very likeable people.

It was another day of conversation in front of the building with a full brigade of gossipers when it happened. On that day, Mrs. Grinjon came angrily looking for her husband. "Where husband?" she demanded of us since she figured we must know. But, unbeknown to us, Mr. Grinjon had been at Stella's apartment for a full week fixing a leak at her kitchen sink. Mrs. Grinjon had finally figured out that one week to fix a leaky faucet didn't add up. She stormed up to Stella's apartment and, like the mob that ran to Frankenstein's castle, we poured into the vestibule of the building to see what would happen. We were not disappointed as we heard splintering wood as Mrs. Grinjon shouldered the door and barged into Stella's apartment. Russian curses, English screams of surprise and more Russian calls for mercy were intermingled with the punches that were being exchanged between husband and wife. Within moments, three arm swinging and shouting forms spilled out of the apartment and came toward the front stoop. First came Mr. Grinjon in undershirt, red striped boxer shorts and socks with no shoes, followed by the arm flailing, clenched fists of Mrs. Grinjon and lastly, Stella clad in pink, see- through, baby doll pajamas. The latter was shouting out in a panic with undecipherable sounds as the Grinjons traded punches on the stoop and on to the sidewalk in front of a throng of onlookers.

The police were called and had a very difficult time in trying to separate the two pugilists and in trying to bring Stella to a safe distance. The end of the day saw the sun set on three disheveled, bruised, beaten and perhaps very embarrassed individuals. At least Stella seemed to be.

Sometimes we were treated to the presence of an important or famous person who would pass by the front stoop on the way home to one of the few wealthy high rise , doorman buildings that dotted East End Avenue. One such person was the famous actor Don Ameche who lived very close by. Mr. Ameche would attend Mass at Saint Steven's Church on east 82nd Street and would pass by always well dressed and polite as he would tip his hat to our mothers and greeted us kids in friendly fashion. Another famous person, Arthur Godfrey, radio show host and amateur banjo player, lived in yet another high-rise building around the corner. He was known for never "tipping" any of the delivery boys or workers who came to his door. His demeanor differed greatly from Mr. Ameche and needless to say, he was not liked. Basil Rathbone, of Sherlock Holmes fame, was known as a gentleman. My mother and I had occasions to meet him as he walked his dog on the John Finley promenade that was directly over the FDR Drive.

There were a few bars in the neighborhood well known to all for the collection of usual suspects who frequented them and were either unemployed or were reluctantly waiting employment while hoping to hit the big one at the racetrack or at the numbers.

My mother and I had to pass by one particular bar on 80th Street and York Avenue on a daily basis as she brought me to school. As we approached the establishment, she would squeeze my hand and pull me quickly along so that I could not get a good look in its dark interior. From 7:00AM to 2:00AM, this watering hole hosted the same red faces with blood- shot eyes whose only sparkle came from a freshly filled glass of shellac -like whiskey as it came into their shaking grips. Once, one of the regulars, dressed in what vaguely resembled an undershirt and pants, spilled out of the front door and shouted a slurred remark through his toothless orifice: "Hey! Look at that tomato!" The poor girl to whom this shout was addressed ran for her life to escape the reach of the outstretched arms of the drunken, stumbling patron. "Mom, why did that man call that lady a tomato?" I asked. "Never mind that." She mumbled as she pulled me away from the scene.

We were poor, didn't have a dime, but were lucky to be a part of the rich fabric of this diverse urban setting.

CHAPTER 3

Tenement Dwelling And Other Stories

WE LIVED A Spartan existence. Tenement apartments were small, hot in the summer, cold in the winter. Toilets were in the hall, bathtubs were in the kitchen. Toilets were shared with other tenants but fortunately not the bathtub which, at dinnertime, served the double purpose of becoming the kitchen table. A metal cover would be placed over the bathtub and voila', dinner would be served. The last room in the "railroad style" apartment (so named because all the rooms connected to each other in the fashion of a railroad car) was the living room that had the only source of heat. A small kerosene stove was it. This room also sported a floor standing radio that always broadcasted a baseball game or operatic music. My grandfather would sit in the dark with a green visor plastic beak hat much like a croupier, smoke cigars, listen to the music and spit in the dark. He never missed the spittoon which was located a few feet from him and his expectorations would land with a sonorous "plunk". Sunday nights meant radio shows, "The Shadow", "Jack Benny", "Amos and Andy",

"Suspense" and others. This was my grandparent's apartment on East 79th Street where I spent many hours since my mother, divorced, was always working. My mother and I lived in a much smaller apartment on the top floor of a five-floor walk up under a tarred roof on which you could fry eggs in the summer. My friend Jeanette and I had an escape, the fire escape. It was our relief on sweltering days. We would climb out of our bedroom window and sit on its scorching metal grid, me on the fifth floor and she on the fourth. Here we would trade comic books. I would lower a rope with a clothespin attached to its end through the fire escape opening down to her floor. She would attach the comic book agreed upon in the trading and I would hoist it up. This we would do for hours but it was never a fair trade. Jeanette, being three years younger was always easily duped. I would take her comic and not send her mine. Needless to say, tears and screams would ensue and send our mothers to the windows and, most of the time, after great turmoil, I would return the comic to its rightful owner .We were both only children but we behaved like the typical brother and sister who beat each other up one minute and defended and protected each other from any outside challenges the next. For all, the fire escape was the extension of the small tenement apartments. Housewives would shake out their dust mops or string laundry out to dry on clotheslines that spanned the length of the interior courtyards or air out beddings. Life was lived in the street , on the fire escape and, as little as possible, in the apartments.

Another escape from the tenement apartments was the school. All of the younger kids in the neighborhood attended PS 158 located on 77th Street and York Avenue, one of the oldest schools of the city. There, the teaching staff ruled with an iron hand over classes of 35 or more students. Desks and seats were bolted to the wooden floors and there we sat in our assigned seats for the entire school year. The teachers, which to me, seemed like old harpies, would leave us in the classroom unattended for one half hour at a time. In their absence not a peep was uttered and no one dared to leave their bolted seats. Our yellowed, dogeared books contained the most deadly boring content matter from which we would dutifully read aloud while standing in a "round robin" fashion going around the room. The boredom was only alleviated when a poor student whose turn had come to read did not have the right place on the page. All attention was focused on what punishment would be swiftly delivered. Our books were assigned once a year and it was our responsibility to cover and care for them. As old as the books were, if our books were marked or destroyed in any way, immediate restitution had to be made followed by a hard rap on the knuckles administered by the harpies with a long, wooden ruler as part payback. Written communication between teachers and students was conducted via the blackboard anchored in the front of the classroom. Assignments and lessons were written on its well-used surface with screeching chalk and dutifully copied in our black and white marbled notebooks. Whacking sounds of rulers or wooden pointers against a non-compliant head delivered with all the skill of a Samurai warrior, delivered the message of punitive intent. A missing or incomplete homework assignment was dealt with in similar fashion. There were three classes on each grade with students grouped according to ability but, despite or because of this, no frill, physically interactive instruction, even the bottom or "dummy class" read on grade.

The school had no gym so physical education classes consisted of being allowed to run like wild madmen for a period of twenty to thirty minutes twice a week in the schoolyard, that is, if we behaved and completed all of our assignments. The girls jumped rope and the boys wrestled or played punch ball. The less adventurous found corners of the yard and either played "split top" or flipped baseball cards or other bubble gum collected cards. Split top was a game where one's wood top was put on the ground and the other players had to try to split it with the metal point of their tops by flinging them on the ground.

The tedium of the daily instructions was relieved by the weekly assembly which occurred following a strict code of behavior. We marched into the auditorium in single file, girls on one side, boys on the other and took our assigned seats, all in absolute silence of course. The dress code was strictly enforced. A white shirt and tie and a white handkerchief were mandatory for the boys. Girls filed in with long skirts, white socks and shoes, tennis shoes i.e. sneakers were not allowed. They mostly wore saddle shoes that were all the rage at the time. The pedagogues of the "old guard" were wise in their choice of long skirts for the girls. The boys, including me, would find some object like a pencil to drop on the floor and give the pretext to bend down and while crawling on the floor, look up the girls' skirts.

As the color guard marched in, everyone stood and saluted the American flag and sang God Bless America and the Star Spangled Banner. Heaven help anyone not standing straight or singing. Many a slap rang out on a student's skull if he were slouching or not singing at the top of his voice. These acts of patriotism were usually followed by speeches on correct behavior or other such topics delivered by the Principal.

Another break in the monotony of droned instructions were the air raid drills. These were the 1950's, the height of the cold war. A siren would sound and we would all file into the hallway and hug the walls. When a signal was sounded, we would drop to the floor and roll up like pill bugs. It was never explained to us how this would save us.

More instructions were delivered to us via a loudspeaker that hung precariously from the plaster walls of our classroom. Periodic addresses from the Principal would bellow forth with reminders of the school rules or other related announcements. Occasionally, an important radio message from President Eisenhower would also be broadcast.

This was a long lasting education which stuck to your ribs. Many years later, I would still duck or cringe whenever I heard clapping or cracking sounds but I can tell you that I certainly learned to read on grade.

But our real education began after school. As we aged up to the sixth grade ,my friends and I would meet up with the sixth grade girls and, if we got lucky, we conned some of them to go with us into the alleyways of the suburban apartments complex sprawled from78th to 79th Street and between York and East End Avenue. The buildings were separated by alleyways navigated by us, by the girls or some bum seeking refuge and a toilet facility. There, we would kiss them, the girls, that is, and try our luck for a quick feel. Later on we would compare notes. If some of us got to feel a thigh or , more rarely, a buttock, it was cause for a celebration and some boasting, of course.

Some of the girls would hang out at one of the more liberated girls' apartment, especially during cold weather. Linda lived on 1st Avenue and 79th Street in a first floor rail road apartment. So, on cold days, after school, we would trade the alleyways for Linda's place and continue our explorations in the last room of the railroad apartment while her parents hung out in the kitchen.

Games like "spin the bottle" and "post office" were the favorites. Of course each game was designed to have someone kiss someone else. At times we would spin a 45 of "doo wop" songs on a small record player in an attempt to get the girls to dance. We danced and, while dancing, tried to "feel up" our dance partners. The girls always removed our hands from certain areas but allowed us to continue our roaming until a critical area was reached. Kissing, even without the cover of a game, was not off limits. We would also lie on top of the girls and roll around a bit while remaining fully dressed , of course. By today's standards, these were pretty tame rites of passage but it was our world of the 1950's.

The Tenements

Public domain photo from the Internet

CHAPTER 4

Little Bastards

WE WERE A disparate bunch of friends when we originally earned the moniker of "little bastards" in elementary school. But, as we moved up through the grades and continued into college and morphed into "The "Hellion's Motorcycle Club", the "little" no longer applied but the "bastards" certainly did.

Harry, the most physically imposing of our core group, stood six feet tall by fifth grade. His blond, curly hair, pale blue eyes, massive shoulders and easy smile masked a wicked sense of humor that would come at you with the force of a speeding train. Harry lived in the Suburban Apartment Complex with his divorced mother, a younger brother and a younger sister. Like many of our mothers, she worked at various jobs but with her janitorial role in the buildings, was able to keep her family afloat. Harry's family was Jewish which was problematic in a neighborhood that sported many "bunt" clubs during and after WWII.

Harry was the most enterprising of us all. He always managed to find part- time employment after school and on weekends. It was Harry who got me my first after school job at the local kosher butcher shop. We could only get working papers at age 14 but at that time, this small detail did not matter.

Little Roger, the smallest of our hard core group was nicknamed "Beechito" meaning "little insect" in Spanish but also "little dick" as slang in some Spanish cultures. This of course, was cause for great merriment at his expense. He was the youngest of the group by about three years but would have done anything to be part of the group. The way Harry was book smart and academically gifted, Roger was a mechanical genius. There was nothing he couldn't fix, from a broken bike to a transistor radio. He was a mechanical genius but sucked at academics.

Like most of us, Roger had an after school job, his was at a neighborhood chicken market named Murrey's. Murrey sold live chickens that were slaughtered and processed on site and sold as "kosher". Roger's job was plucking the dead chickens, cleaning the cages, sweeping and hosing down the grimy floors. Needless to say he took a lot of teasing over the years including clucking sounds whenever he approached the group. As one of four siblings, he came from the largest family of our group. Angelo, his father, a hard working man, only came home to fall out after doing double and triple shifts at his handyman jobs. Roger's mother was into interior decorating and would change the apartment's curtains and furniture as often as changing underwear, hence Angelo's three work shifts. Roger had a fiery temper that could burst out when least expected. Once, for whatever reason he deemed fit, he chased me through his railroad apartment wielding a twelve inch butcher knife with all the intent of using it on me. At that time I escaped serious damage to life and limb by grabbing one of his sisters and hurling her in his path, thus derailing his trajectory.

Marc was the philosopher and the scholar of the group. He had a serious nature and needed much coaxing to get him into a jocular mood. Marc had two sisters and a mother and a father but even though they all shared the same small apartment, his parents lived a life outside the family. I guess you could say they lived a bohemian life style. His father was a good but unknown painter, his mother was a good but unknown writer and the kids were part of the accouterment. At a young age, Marc helped to support his family by working long hours in his grandmother's dry cleaning business. I guess that was the arrangement. He would work in the shop and the grandmother would subsidize the family. Consequently Marc was always tired, sporting dark circles under his eyes and dozing off in class. Throughout the seasons he could be seen wearing a long, flowing grey coat. This too became a source of teasing as we would say that he looked like Chief Geronimo wrapped up in a blanket. Of course, that was why Roger became Beechito and Marc became "Chiefcoat".

I was the oldest of this motley crew. With a grandfather from Caguas, Puerto Rico, a grandmother from Palermo, Italy and a father with Danish and Irish roots I was the poster child of this multi ethnic neighborhood . At times, the conflict among the various ethnicities would spill out into our home. My grandfather whose job was to roll cigars was rabidly proud to be a Puerto Rican and one day, when a fellow worker expressed his views that all Puerto Rican women were ugly, my grandfather went after him with the metal roller he used on his cigars. He did not inflict too much damage but unfortunately his job went up in smoke. From that time to his dying days he sat in his little apartment listening to Caruso records and smoking cigars. My grandmother was a little lady with beautiful peaches and cream complexion and long auburn hair, a legacy from the Nors invasion of Sicily. She kept the small family afloat by sewing beads onto fancy garments that she could never afford. My mother, an only child, was rebellious and perhaps a bit ashamed of her ethnic roots and spent most of her time on he street with friends or days on end in the homes of her Jewish friends. She married young and unfortunately for my father, he was her ticket out of her household. A worse match could not have been planned. She was wild, loved dancing and friends. He was subdued and introspective. The marriage lasted four years and I was the end product of this unfortunate union. All of us, Marc. Harry, Roger and me shared in the reality of a missing or un-involved father which ,I believe, helped to sow the seeds for our misdeeds.

I grew up fast and was about 6' by sixth grade. Harry was massive and perhaps that's why he was never given a nick-name. I, on the other hand, had long legs hence my nick-name "Legs Artie". It could have been worse. All of us Just like the rest of the guys I worked after school and on weekends. Thanks to Harry I delivered meat from Gene's Butcher shop. Tips weren't good but I was making a dollar an hour which wasn't bad for that time. The local stores offered a lot of op-portunity for deliveries to the high-rise buildings with their af-fluent tenants. The liquor store, the stationary shop, the florist ,and the dry cleaners all were part of my employment history.

Each season had its own repertoire of material. The cold brought us inside and the warm weather, outside. Each of the following venues served as our stage of horrors –libraries, schools, restaurants, movie theaters, parks, museums, depart-ment stores, buses, trains, and eventually motorcycles.

Some of the gags were truly humorous and all of the ones written in this book are true. In today's world, our merriment would have brought bullets or other harsh forms of retribution. I'm sure that those victims of our actions are waiting anxiously on the other side ready to give us our due.

One of our early escapades as a group began in early elementary school. We would sneak into school after 3P.M. when only a few teachers stayed behind to attend to classwork. Our target was the refrigerator in the lunchroom. It , having been left unlocked, would contain ice cream and peanut butter sandwiches. Our days of "food gathering" came to a halt when the custodian, Mr. Butterfield, caught us in the act and threatened to beat us senseless. We wormed our way out of that mess by using our infinite charm- begging for mercy.

Three o'clock meant freedom for us and the beginning of suffering for those in our path of "merrymaking." One of our targets used to be the Green Kitchen on 77th street and 1st avenue. It is still there and is operating very well. The kitchen was located on the side of the restaurant around the corner from the front entrance. A plain door led to the small kitchen and cook with his assistants. We would open the door and shout obscenities and then would bravely run away. As we got closer to sixth grade, our minds cooked up more complicated scenarios.

Above the door was a fan, an old fashioned one with three blades which, when inactive in colder weather , was motionless. We found that small stones and other debris could, with the proper aim, pass through the small space between the fan blades. There was always a giant pot of soup under the fan which rested on a shelf. Of course we tried to pass debris through the blades on a daily basis and on one particular day, our aims were true.

The missiles were thrown and they passed through the blades. The door opened and the angry cook armed with a ladle exited the kitchen and we ran. He was of average height and perhaps middle age and he wore a black moustache. His look was unmistakably Greek. His loud and clear accent confirmed his ethnicity as he shouted "my soup, my soup." We ran for about one block and he , being out of breath, finally had to give up the chase and stop. Our sides ached with laughter and also pained from the running.

CHAPTER 5

Another Candy Store

HIS COFFEE STAINED excuses for teeth parted and a gust of foul breath escaped from the rotten orifice which could liberally called a mouth. A thoroughly chewed cigar moved in rhythm with his speech pattern as he bellowed, "yes?"

He was known as AB, the proprietor of a filthy candy store on York Avenue and 80th Street. He stood about 5 feet and was proportioned like an Easter Egg. His eyebrows were thick and extremely long which added a presence of evil or mystery where there was none. His manner was rough and his chores consisted of chasing away the flies which used the exposed sweets as a landing strip and cursing away the customers , mostly kids who easily parted with their penny in exchange for the tainted "goodies" that AB displayed.

He kept a broom behind the counter which was used as a weapon when some of the eight year olds became aggressive. Not withstanding, his place provided a momentary respite from the daily routine and a sense of adventure since he became quite adept at swinging his broom.

Many a rock found its mark from the hands of the youths who were his customers. One could say that at the end of the day, the broom and the missiles that reached its target , his head, were in a dead draw.

Places like AB's in the neighborhood provided the social center for children and young teens. Being mostly a street corner society, these stores were vital to the hangoutees and to the financial existence of their proprietors.

There were many "toughs" in Yorkville at the time. These gangster types hung together and had no desire to socialize with us and, vice versa. Our only interaction with them was the occasional "shakedowns" in which they would take whatever coins that were found in our pockets. Some of these "sterling" citizens later went on to fill the ranks of some prison or worse.

There were always gangs in Yorkville and the 1950's saw no change. Most times, locals were not bothered by these marauders. There were many apartment robberies even though people felt comfortable in leaving their doors unlocked.

CHAPTER 6

The Little Bastards At The Library And The Movie Houses

SEVENTY NINTH STREET and 1st Avenue was a very heavily populated intersection. There were banks on the opposite corners and a coffee shop named Riker's (not to be confused with Riker's Island which houses prisoners).The cooks employed there should have been sent to Riker's Island as punishment for their poor culinary skills.

We four, and other anxious confederates, of elementary school age, would station ourselves on the street corner and hurl various objects at the traffic and at the pedestrians. We once found old 78R.P.M. records which were made of shellac and possessed excellent flight patterns when thrown correctly. We were ahead of our time since Frisbees were not yet in production. We would aim at people that were scurrying to and fro on the opposite side of the avenue. These flat saucers, when thrown, would accelerate rapidly and were probably more dangerous than we thought.

When we were bored or cold, we went to one of the neighborhood libraries where we quickly became known. One of our pranks included assimilating with the library patrons at the reading and reference tables. We would prop up a large text chosen at random which served as a kind of shield. Armed with straws purloined from the school cafeteria, we rolled up and wet paper balls which were used as our artillery. We would spread out

(sometimes many as ten of us) and select a target. This was usually a person that was reading a book or beginning to fall asleep.

We never bothered the elderly, infirm, women or children. This was our code born of either a false sense of chivalry or a heightened sense for danger. Upon a signal from one in our group, the rest would fire at the chosen victim and we would all "duck" under the large books that barricaded us from view. Of course our presence was soon detected and complaints were lodged with the librarian. She was an elderly woman with white hair and spectacles with a demeanor like George Washington's as he froze crossing the Delaware.

Thus began the first of many ejections from the library. Fortunately for us there was another library on East 79th Street and 3rd Avenue. This backup locale provided us with another opportunity at carrying out the same antics. Of course, we were thrown out of there too.

The movie houses were the perfect places for our devilry. The large dark interiors provided a perfect backdrop for us. We would begin in the bathrooms that were located down a winding flight of stairs. Long carpeted steps led to a large area with urinals and at least five stalls for more serious business. Each one had a door which closed for privacy and a sit down toilet. We would wait for someone to enter one of the stalls or, if we were lucky, all of them would be filled to capacity. Our weapons were cups filled with water which we hurled over the top of the door and which struck the poor soul that was sitting on the bowl. A good aim was not necessary and the guy on the receiving end became drenched with water.

There was always cursing along with threats on our lives from the victim. Of course we knew that we were safe from punishment considering what the person was doing inside.

Once up the stairs, we would purchase various kinds of hard candies from the food counter and make our way into the darkened interior. The hard spheres were hurled at random and sometimes found its mark as loud screams provided proof as such. Sometimes, from the balcony area , we would drop large cups of water or fire paper clips from a tense rubber band onto the moviegoers below. Eventually, our presence would be discovered and we would run clumsily while laughing uncontrollably and head for another movie house on 86th street.

There were four movie houses on East 86th street between 3rd and Lexington Avenue. Relatively, theater prices were much cheaper than they are today. This provided us the opportunity to go movie hopping whenever we were ejected from one of the others.

CHAPTER 7

Regular Visitors
In The Neighborhood

THE RINGING BELLS of the approaching junkman was a regularly heard sound on our streets. His entire business was refuse and garbage that he rummaged through and probably sold somewhere for a few coins.

His vehicle was an old wagon without a top , much like the one used in the Ma and Pa Kettle films. An old horse slowly pulled the rig and a series of bells on a rope and tied along a pole that covered the length of the wagon, sounded his arrival.

Our mothers would fill the wagon with old newspapers , rags, and unwanted clothes. The empty soda bottles were off limits as they were used by us kids to bring to the supermarket for a two cents reward on each.

He would nod his head in appreciation and to the children he was like some mysterious folk hero. Did he have a family? What was his name? Was he as old as he looked? Could he survive without that wagon and horse?

Another regular was the tool sharpener who would push an old wagon and sharpen our parents' knives and scissors. People that milled around the stoops would run up to their apartments when he came by and would bring down their dull tools for him to sharpen.

During the 1940s and early 1950s, most of us did not have refrigerators. Small metal boxes placed on the window sill or other shelf area , were filled with large pieces of ice. These " ice boxes" served as our refrigerators.

Once a week, a truck would pull up in front of a group of buildings and a short, powerful, swarthy individual with a heavy Italian accent would shout in an almost operatic voice, "Ice a man, ice a man."

For 25 cents, a piece of ice was chopped and wrapped inside of an old filthy towel and lifted onto his shoulder. He would run up the stairs with the ice and place it in the metal box where it lasted for a few days and slowly melt away.

He usually came by on Saturday mornings and was a welcome sight. We did not realize the importance of his arrival as the ice would preserve our food for at least three days.

Other regular appearances in the neighborhood were the strolling musicians. We would sit on the fire escapes that faced the backyard and wait for the sour serenades.

These musicians, generously labeling them such, would stroll the "grounds" and bang out a dreadful interpretation of some once beautiful standard tune. One of the regular groups consisted of an Alto Saxophonist , a Violinist , and a third who gathered up whatever coins that were hurled in their direction.

The Hare Krishna would come in a poor second to this group's persistence. To accelerate their departure, we would wrap some low denomination coins in tissue paper and throw them towards the musicians. The money was quickly scooped up and they eventually left.

Street Musicians

Public domain picture from the Internet

The fire escapes served as platforms for our mothers to stand on and hang the wash(always done by hand) on two parallel moving ropes called wash or clothes lines. These were anchored with a kind of pulley at the end and fastened onto a protruding nail and with wooden clothes pins, the wet garments would be sent by rope on their way to be dried. Everyone saw everyone else's laundry right down to the underwear.

CHAPTER **8**

Let's Go To The
Department Store

THROUGHOUT OUR JUNIOR High and High School days, we became more mobile and our choice of venues was extended from the immediate neighborhood into other parts of the city.

Our "reign of terror" added some peripheral members from adjoining streets, but these new initiates came and went at the first sign of trouble or a police presence.

Some of the most memorable gags took place in the large department stores in midtown Manhattan. These included Bloomingdale's , Macy's, Abercrombie and Fitch, Sacks Fifth Avenue, and others.

On Saturday afternoons, Harry W. and I would venture on foot from our meeting point on east 79th street and work our way through the city causing whatever improvised mayhem that we could conjure at the moment.

We would ride the escalators and came up with a neat plan. We "borrowed" a bow with rubber tipped arrows from the sporting goods department and aimed these arrows at men who sported hats as they rode either up or down. For example, if we were riding up, we would fire at some guy with a hat who was going down or vice versa. On occasion, our aims were true and the hapless victim would find his hat flying off of his head. Of course, everyone else on the crowded escalator had a good laugh at the expense of the "target."

My sides have ached from laughing on many an occasion while thinking about one of our antics in the large department stores on West 34th street. I don't remember the store's name (perhaps Stearn's) but, it was near Macy's.

We rode the escalator to the second floor that housed a large section that contained all of the latest radios, televisions, and amplifiers. These all used glass tubes unlike today's computer chips and circuit boards technology and it took many seconds for the tubes to warm up before working. We calculated the distance from the display area to the down escalator and figured that if we turned on a row of radios and televisions full blast, we had a gambler's chance of making our hasty retreat without apprehension.

And so we began, in dead earnest, to turn on as many TVs, radios, and amplifiers as was possible in a short time span. We knew that the warm-up before the symphony of cacophony would begin, was just a matter of seconds.

Naturally, as always, we ran like devils to the nearest escalator and were rewarded with a blast of sound from the displays which sent salesmen and shoppers alike into a frenzy. Some people screamed and others ran in place as panic stricken salesmen first tried to locate the exact area of noise and then tried to silence the bellowing instruments.

We stood by the top of the escalator crying with laughter and grabbed onto our already paining stomachs.

CHAPTER 9

The Trains

THE ABOVE GROUND train which was known as the "Third avenue El " ran uptown and downtown atop 3rd avenue on regular railroad tracks which were supported by stone pillars that were embraced by the street below. Traffic could run its normal course on the ground between the huge supports and rail commuters rode 20 feet or more above the ground.

On some Saturdays, my grandmother and I would ride the El going downtown to the factory where she worked and then home again on the tracks which ran on the opposite side. She would ask if I wanted to go with her on the El and I would jump with joy at the prospect of riding on the trains. This was in the 1950's and I was about seven years old. She would take me by the hand and we would walk from East 79th street where she lived to the station at 77th street and 3rd avenue.

I remember that it was so exciting to wait on the platform and look for the arrival of the slow moving train. The trains and the platforms were very clean and vandalism was almost non existent. The stations had penny vending machines which were in good condition. For a penny, one could buy gum and candy. The interior of the trains had hard straw seats which were not the most comfortable and above them hung leather straps set in porcelain anchors which afforded passengers not lucky enough to secure a seat, something to hang onto.

Subway rides cost five cents and there were thick wooden turnstiles which were very hard to push. They were fun for us because we made a game out of pushing them around like wheels.

The train- cars were free of debris and of course graffiti , which was an unknown phenomenon in those days, was non-existent. No one dared even think of marking or defacing the trains. The sense of community pride was a very strong tenet in our neighborhoods. Blue collar or not, people honored and respected the law.

I can recall being on the El with my grandmother when a man lit a cigarette. The entire trainload of passengers shouted out their indignation causing him to immediately extinguish it.

Men would readily give up their seats for a woman or elderly passenger. I never even thought twice about giving up my seat for a lady. My grandfather, of old school thought, used to tip his hat if a woman were in front of him. This was ordinary behavior and good manners were expected.

The ride on the El would afford the passengers a grand view of the tenements that lined the avenue. We took for granted what is now seen in photos that fill books on New York City history.

Second and Third avenue were not exactly places that were listed on high society party invitation lists. These streets were saturated with all kinds of Mom and Pop stores and vendors galore. Population density was high and the average family income was low. Yet, the streets were relatively safe and the handful of hoboes that peppered the area were known and were harmless.

The Third Avenue L

Public domain picture from the Internet

CHAPTER 10

Terror On The Bus

PUBLIC TRANSPORTATION , especially buses served as excellent sites for many a prank. We liked to ride the ones that went all the way downtown and returned to our point of origin. One could board on 2nd avenue and return with the 3rd or 5th avenue lines.

One of our bright ideas involved bringing plastic straws and bags of beans on board. Once having secured a window seat and having raised the window to the top, the world was our target practice.

On one warm evening, the cast of characters included Harry_____, Roger_____, and myself. We secured our window seats and began to set up our fortress. The flying peas would strike an innocent pedestrian and the stinging sensation would force the person to automatically shout or even to jump . Imagine someone walking along in the crowd as he is struck by flying peas. The other pedestrians had no way of knowing that he was struck by these hard orbs. Seeing a person jump or shout out without apparent provocation was unsettling to those that travelled in his wake.

Passengers on the bus saw what we were doing and vicariously joined in the fun with laughter caused by the suffering of another stranger.

Upon returning uptown on the 5th avenue line, we were given a great opportunity. The bus had stopped for traffic and we faced some large windows of the many beautiful stores that were part of the 5th avenue scene. Standing in front of a large window were two well dressed men with their backs to us. We unleashed a volley of peas with great force. Some of the peas struck the window and ricocheted onto the two men. Others found their mark and struck them on all parts of their body. Almost as if by instinct, the duo fell to the ground in perfect synchronization and lay flat, much like a scene from an Elliot Ness and the Untouchables film.

Those passing by stood in shock in the belief that they had been shot execution style. As the men rose to their feet , our laughter could not be contained. We hastily closed the windows and the two banged at the window with clenched fists and shouted curses and threats of retaliation.

Naturally, we trembled with fear and prayed that the bus would soon begin its journey once again. As it did, the duo ran alongside the bus, cursing and threatening us. A few blocks later, they abandoned their chase and continued shaking their fists at us.

CHAPTER 11

Culture At The Museum

ONE OF OUR most frequently visited places was the world famous Metropolitan Museum Of Art located on 81st street and 5th avenue. An unknowing observer would be led to believe that we were the most cultured group of teens in the city. These museum visits became more and more frequent with time.

The Museum is a very large structure with rows of cement stairs in front. People, mostly tourists, sit atop them and read, talk, eat , or just relax. The many halls and rooms inside host some of the world's greatest paintings and exhibits.

The museum venture began during our High School years. Our sojourns continued on an almost weekly schedule until the guards finally banded together and threatened us with bodily harm if we were to return.

The highlight of our visitations took place on a Sunday afternoon,the most crowded day at the museum. Once past the entrance, there is a large lobby area and straight ahead are rows of stone stairs 30 feet long and numbering about forty. At the top , there used to be a large water fountain where people would stand by and talk, catch their breaths, and occasionally toss all denominations of coins. We noticed that there was a considerable amount of cash awaiting our procurement and hatched our plan.

We decided to remove our shoes and socks , rolled up our pants , and entered the fountain. We immediately began scooping the coins from their underwater resting place and stuffed them into our pockets. The already present crowd gathered round and stood in shocked silence as we laughed and frolicked in the water. Our revelry was interrupted by the arrival of a very big black guard who upon seeing what was unfolding, clapped his hands twice, signaling a call to arms for the other guards.

Before this large, dumbfounded audience, at least 10 uni-formed men grabbed us bodily and roughly removed us from the fountain. They ordered us to remove the cache of coins from our pockets and began pushing us towards the top of the stairs and down to the exit. The odds were heavily against us to consider initiating a round of fisticuffs and we exited the fountain without further incident. Of course we had to throw back almost all of the catch as Marc_____ managed to keep some of it.

The gathered crowd laughed at this burlesque with our quartet of soaked pants, and bare feet throwing back coins into the fountain, its rightful owner. We were not done with our mu-seum antics as we planned to add more wise guys in the future.

The future came quickly as a herd of us would run through the galleries shouting and mocking the guards. These "senti-nels" followed us wherever we went and would try to nip in the bud our next move. These guards didn't appreciate our brand of humor that include mock plans spoken so that we would be overheard as to how we were going to spray paint the famous paintings at first opportunity.

Finally, one day saw the angry crew of guards greeted us at the door and for a while at least, that was it.

CHAPTER 12

The Four Little Bastards

THE EVENINGS FOUND an average of twenty teens huddled on one of the stoops chosen in the middle of 81st street. This loose confederation would wile away the time with talk of sex, sex, and sex. Everyone made claims to some misadventure with the opposite sex which were, blown out of proportion or mere fabrications.

Robert_____, one of the stoop hangers, was observed to disappear at almost always the same time. Physical pressure made him disclose his daily routine of watching the female occupant in the apartment across the street as she paraded nude in front of her window. We managed to extract a schedule of this grand event including many of the delicious details. Robert_____ must be given credit as he held out his confession for a long time but, the blows to his skull proved to be his downfall as the relief of pain for information was a good trade.

Luck was with us one evening as Robert_____ unwillingly pointed to her arriving at the entrance to her building as he declared, "that's her." The pack of twenty some odd delinquents charged the staircase and noisily fought for the best vantage point at the edge of the roof. We were given a schedule of events that would shortly take place in the woman's apartment.

She would enter the apartment and sit down to enjoy a glass of milk and cookies. She then would partially undress and relax for a bit.

Our heartbeats could be heard on Mars as the anticipation built. An almost unbearable length of time passed as our hostess drew a bath and prepared to remove the rest of her garments.

Robert's information proved to be true right down to the most minute detail. We later found that Robert had created a schedule of her daily routines that would have made NASA mission control proud. She entered the bathroom and a quick view of her splendid body caused us to gasp pitifully.

The big moment finally arrived as the bathroom door was opened and the beauty exited slowly. A problem developed at this point of our long awaited presentation. The steam from the bath immediately fogged up the windows which, to our dismay, shielded the beauty from our hungry eyes.

A chorus of "boos" from the mouths of the heartbroken onlookers filled the air. We heard loud laughter from a window located across the street. Charlie_____ , an older friend, knew what we were up to and from his vantage point, shined what looked like a police flashlight directly upon us.

With stooped shoulders and dragging feet, we left the roof top very disappointedly. Of course we took out our anger at Robert who, despite being very accurate in every detail, did not deliver the final treat.

CHAPTER 13

High School
And More Pranks

THE HIGH SCHOOL years presented the greatest risk for our "merrymaking." We were older and stronger so the chance of being physically challenged or beaten by the recipients of our chicanery were greater.

We also had some minor brushes with the police where physical punishment was threatened. Police in those days didn't have civilian review boards or anti- police organizations to worry about. Each patrolman was assigned a specific "beat" and keeping order was his call.

Sometimes, a particular patrolman didn't like us hanging out on the stoops and he would take his night stick (a heavy and thick club) and bang it on the steps of our hangout. On one singular evening, a tough cop whacked the steps where we were sitting and shouted, "This stoop is mine." We dared not answer back and we scattered as "asked."

These acts of the law did not in any way temper our desire to continue with our "programs." On the contrary as the omnipresent possibility of physical retaliation by the police just fed our desire to cause mayhem.

Springtime in Central Park proved to be a rich palette and an abundant source of unwilling victims. Everyday after school, we would walk home through the park at West 67th street entrance and find someone to make miserable. Our confederation sometimes numbered up to ten and it was run like an army war maneuver.

One of our plans involved water balloons and of course a breathing target. A large number of balloons were filled at one of the many water fountains that were placed in all parts of the park. We carried large cardboard boxes where we placed our water bombs.

We carefully scouted out an area where there were multiple escape routes. We feared apprehension by one of angry victims.

Park benches were usually chosen as there were always one to a few men seated there enjoying a quiet sunny spring day. Very carefully, we slowly approached the bench from our vantage point being some thick bush or tree. We spread out in a long single line and brandished the water balloons for activation.

One of us was delegated the task of sounding the "commence fire" and a volley of overstuffed rubber spheres of water would be hurled at the unsuspecting victim. I can only imagine the feelings that these human targets must have felt at the exact moment that these missiles of water struck them.

First, the shock of objects on your person, then the large volume of water as it soaked you entirely, then the realization of what had happened followed by the uncontrolled laughter and running feet of the protagonists.

Our bodies pumped with adrenalin as the danger of being pursued was very possible. We also would hurl the balloons from just a few feet from the target. A victim swift of foot could have caught one of us and the beating would of course have commenced.

Winters brought a change in our devilry. We still did, if not more, carry on with the aid of a good snowfall. The throwing of objects was still the focal point of our mischief and what better medium than snow that could be made into excellently formed missiles.

There are two incidents that I still vividly recall with much laughter. On one cold winter night, the four little bastards walked along Lexington Avenue in the area of 65th street looking for a place or persons to practice their devilry. We noticed a man shoveling snow from his car at about 100 feet from the corner. Of course we all had prepared a snowball in his honor. My throw was the most true as the wet sphere struck him squarely on the cheek as he was clearing the snow from the roof of his car.

We laughed, he cursed, and immediately began a hot pursuit which lasted for a few city blocks but seemed interminable. This time I knew that we were in trouble. His large shovel was raised over his head and he was ready to lower it on our heads. I turned my head around for a moment and he looked like a madman. He was shouting, "I'll kill you, you F------ bastards. He was the stuff that nightmares are made of.

Roger and Marc , being the two most fleet of foot of the four were ahead of Harry and I by some ten feet. We two ,being a bit slower than Roger and Marc, were just one pace in front of the angry, expletive driven lunatic with the raised shovel.

My heart beat like a tympani drum at a Saint Vitus dance festival and I think I would have cried out for mercy at any moment. Finally, what seemed to be hours, our young, sweaty, shaking bodies were just too much for the madman and he gave up.

The true "snowball from Hell" came from the hands of Harry on one busy winter day. We were at least six strong and we merrily strolled along Lexington Avenue perusing the store displays and thinking about our next plot.

As we walked along the east side of the avenue, just past one of our favorite stores, Bloomingdale's, an opportunity came our way. A mound of snow which was mostly slush presented itself like an oasis in the vast desert. Harry quickly scooped up a large amount of it and formed a not too perfect snowball. As slushy as it was, it would find its mark somewhere.

On the opposite corner, diagonally across the street from us, a group of people waited impatiently for the traffic light to turn green. As it did, the crowd, like young stallions, rushed from one corner to get to the next save one soul. He seemed to be well dressed at first blush and was probably a bit beyond middle age, well beyond our code of acceptance.

I believe to this day, that he had consumed too many martinis at lunch as he appeared to be standing like Captain Bligh on the high seas.

We taunted Harry to throw his snowball in the direction of this target never believing that it would even reach the vicinity of the tottering form.

Harry was known to not have a good aim. In fact, his aim was terrible. At any rate, he threw the slush ball at this man who was at least 100 feet or better away from us. We had not noticed that this same person was desperately trying to light a cigar at the same time that he was attempting to stand erect.

As the snowball was released, we stared at the vain attempt at the cigar lighting and at the same time, observed the many people scurrying across the intersection. With less of a chance to hit its target than winning the super lotto, the ball of slush and snow cleanly knocked the cigar out of his mouth.

His face was covered with snow and his unlit cigar travelled many feet away. He remained rocking back and forth on the corner probably not believing what had happened or how it happened as we rolled up into balls and convulsed with wild laughter. Just in case though, we ran away.

CHAPTER **14**

The Movies

THE "MOVIES" DREW almost every kid from the neighborhood on Saturday afternoons. Everyone under the age of twelve looked forward all week to either one of the local movie houses. They were the Monroe Theater on 75th street and 1st avenue and the Colony on East 79th street and 2nd avenue where a synagogue now stands in its stead. Of the two, parents preferred the Colony. It had fewer bums, was cleaner, and hosted better behaved kids.

I remember my grandmother surprising me one day when she brought me to the Monroe. It was the first time that the theater hosted the Miss America contest. Bert Parks, that perennial figure was the M.C. of the event.

The Colony featured a Saturday matinee which ran from 9A.M. to 12 noon. It included endless cartoons, news specials, some short presentations, and the main feature that was usually Abbot and Costello or Ma and Pa Kettle.

Unescorted children would have to leave at 12 noon whereupon a double feature and more cartoons were the normal fare. I don't know how my Mother sat with me all day from 9A.M. till 5P.M. up to her knees in refuse such as spilled popcorn, candy boxes, and soda cups.

Some of the children could deftly elude the ushers' flashlights and manage to stay for the later show.

I was allowed to invite a friend on these Saturday marathons. My mother prepared lunches of Brown bread with American cheese and butter and off we went. For five cents, you could hang out all day for the marathon of flicks. One usually left the theater with a large headache and eye strain.

I once saw one of the clerks behind the candy counterwdrop her bracelet in the synthetic butter that was used on the pop corn. She unabashedly went "fishing" for the bracelet with her not so clean hands.

The typical movie house had a large ornate marquis with Black metal letters which were set against a white background, advertising the presentation at that time. After purchasing a ticket, we walked onto a well trodden carpet up to the ticket taker. Ornate columns were everywhere as they clashed with the ushers' uniforms which, with their gaudily decorated epaulets and golden stripes on the pants, resembled the uniforms of some military officers in a third world country.

Upon retrieving your half of the torn ticket stub, you entered a large, dark auditorium and began to search for a vacant seat. An usher with a bright shining flashlight begrudgingly led you to an unoccupied seat . The theaters had declining sloping floors so that if you had to leave your seat for any reason, it gave you the feeling of being at the first level of a stress test.

The rows of seats were on the right and left sides with center rows separated from these by an aisle of about five feet. I remember that there must have been about fifty rows on each side unlike the theaters of today where these large ones have been cut into smaller ones much like renovated apartments.

Long winding and carpeted stairs led to the balcony area which was also filled with many rows that were horizontally separated by steps. Extra entertainment was provided by those patrons who stumbled in the darkness without the assistance of some semi -comatose usher.

Bathrooms were located on a lower level and to reach them, one would have to walk down along a carpeted winding staircase.

The concession stand contained the usual popcorn machine, ice cream freezers, and row upon row of candy. Most of the candies such as JU Jubes, bell shaped and hard and very small, are no longer in existence. Other sweets were Bonamo's Turkish Taffy, Mary Jane bars which unlike today were swollen with peanut butter, Wrigley's chewing gum, Sen Sen tablets to mask tobacco breath, Good and Plenty candies with a sweet hard shell which covered a licorice underneath, Cracker Jacks with prizes on the bottom of the box, and many more.

The refuse of these goodies was usually discarded under the seats which by the end of the day, would form a significant pile.

Those latecomers would invariably step on these empty boxes and left over candies and popcorn and create a sound like castanets which of course was very annoying.

Since children under the age of sixteen would not be admitted without an adult escort, we resorted to begging a stranger to pose as our parent so that we could enter the theater. Once inside, we would be on our own.

Habitually, we would be removed from the theater after a short time for noise making and other mischief that I wrote about earlier. We thought that it was fun to shout out the endings of a mystery film much to the fury of the other patrons.

Part time and weekend employment was grabbed up by the teens in the neighborhood immediately. Some of us held down two or more positions which we juggled into our already busy school schedules.

The butcher shops, florists, druggists, liquor and stationary stores were the most readily available. The movie theaters were the least attractive because as ushers, we would have to dress up with bow ties and jackets and there were no "tips." In addition, the boredom could drive one insane.

The ushers provided mainly simple services and contact with the clientele was almost non existent but for being asked for the time or hearing a complaint in the theater.

Harry and I were able to secure positions as ushers in an upscale movie house on Madison Avenue and East 85th street. It was the Trans Lux Theater. In time, we were able to add another friend, Anthony_____, to the roster.

It was a small theater that catered to the upper crust clientele of the affluent neighborhood. It did not have the grandiose construction of those that we were used to as kids.

There were two managers, one a Mr. Barnstein, a bespectacled , elderly man with a kind demeanor and a Jiminy Cricket like expression. His subordinate, Mr. Bozan (referred to within the employee's circle as Mr. Bozo), was a short pudgy looking middle aged man with a very nervous demeanor and who was always very jittery even in casual conversation.

The other employees were interesting types. There was Rose___ , the ticket taker, a kind of want to be of Street Car Named Desire figure , Blanche DuBois, only much more boring. Jerry____, was the head usher(in more ways than one) . His same sex preference was very noted but he didn't bother us. A confederate of his joined the team later on and his name escapes me. Rounding out the staff was George___, an old cranky black who ran the small concession stand. Another black, a heavy Post Office employee pulling the double shift was Mr. Thomas. He was always pleasant and he always knew about the shenanigans that we were pulling.

Two older gentlemen, Mr. Rich and Mr. Craft , rounded out the motley team. Rich was a nervous, bent over figure who repeated everything that someone said no matter what it was.

Mr. Craft was an alcoholic who always carried a small flask of liquor. He was pleasant and claimed that he knew every word in the dictionary. We once challenged him and he failed miserably.

Once we found a discarded whiskey bottle and urinated in it. We placed it inconspicuously in the employees' bathroom in full view. We waited for Mr. Craft to enter and watched him through the partially opened door. He raised the bottle to his quivering lips but smelled piss and put it down.

The ladies' dressing room was located directly below ours. We knew when Rose took her dinner break and hung a very heavy and long coat (much like one that Napoleon sported in his portraits) over the light bulb that hung from the ceiling. It looked like a person hanging from the ceiling. This detested coat was used by us when we had to serve as "Barkers" outside of the theater announcing the time of the next film presentation. It was long and heavy and had grotesque epaulets on the shoulders. The large fake gold buttons were comedic. The coat seemed to weigh 100 pounds.

We sneaked the hated garment into the ladies' dressing room, shaking with laughter in anticipation of what was going to happen. We unscrewed the light bulb in the corner of the room and loosened the other one that hung from the ceiling. The faint bulb created an eerie setting for our scheme.

We hung the coat under the diminished bulb. Of course we waited for a full house and then took up our posts at the rear of the theater.

Rose slowly opened the door to her room and began to scream uncontrollably. The patrons rustled about in fear of the shrieking that was coming from Rose. "There's a man hanging, there's a man hanging" she bellowed as she ran up the aisle. Moviegoers stood up, some in panic, and of course the three of us laughed.

It was nervous Bozan to the rescue and Mr. Thomas put the lights on. The film was halted and we came running down the aisle in mock surprise. Bozan knew that we had done it but could not prove it. Rose stopped talking to us for good.

There were metal side doors which served as alternate or emergency exits and were seldom used. We found a use for them , however.

On Friday evenings, we would open the doors to Marc who worked in his father's tailor shop just a few blocks away. Roger, after a day of plucking chickens at his place of work, Murrey's Kosher Chickens, came by also. The four were re-united for an evening of "merriment."

It began with very innocuous mischief like shining our flashlights on bald patrons' heads from the balcony area. The other moviegoers laughed at the expense of the bald person as he sat in the dark unknowingly.

The usual throwing of candies or other objects continued and often found their mark thanks to years of practice. We set up traps in the mens' room such as leaving the inner door opened at a 45 degree angle. The outer door would strike the second one and yield a force that would cause the person entering to be forced backwards, just enough to cause surprise followed by cursing.

Siamese to the doors was a water fountain with a paper cup dispenser that held a few dozen cone shaped paper cups. We found that if we pulled the bottom cup down, just at the point of removing it from the stack, and filling it halfway with water and then carefully replacing it on the bottom, it would squirt water all over the person that went to pull it out.

Once, when the film "Psycho" was being shown,(this was years after it had debuted in theaters) Anthony _____ chased me down the dark aisle with the Fireman's ax that was stored for emergency at the rear of the theater shouting, "Psycho."

People screamed and we ran back to our posts. The patrons didn't know what was going on. Bozan came in as he heard the screams from the lobby and saw us standing at attention in the rear of the auditorium. He knew but didn't know, at least , not yet.

Trans Lux was proud to present a premier performance of the film "The Young Doctors" starring Frederic March. Large crowds showed up to this relatively small movie house and we were drilled as how to do crowd control, etc.

Mr. Bozan, the paper general, came up with a plan that would allow people entering and exiting to do so in an orderly fashion. We three were told to be prepared to open the seldom used emergency doors upon his signal, to allow the patrons to leave the theater as the new arrivals could enter without causing a traffic jam. This was for once, sound logic on his part as the movie house was small and large crowds were expected. The ushers proved to be the fly in the ointment of his plan.

At about 15 minutes to zero hour, as we synchronized watches and made ready our hour, I found that I was alone on the floor. Harry and Anthony were not to be found. I had not been told of the scheme that they had hatched.

The audience was led by Bozan and brought to line up at the exit doors. The newly arrived crowd was held back by the head usher Jerry on the side behind rope barriers. I was waiting for Bozan's signal to open the side doors when I saw Harry and Anthony enter from one of the last emergency doors, just feet from the nervous Bozan and moviegoers who now just wanted to exit as soon as possible.

Like horses in place at the starting gate, the crowd began to press against me as I stood with my back to the doors .Bozan signaled and I opened the doors. I could not believe what I saw and simultaneously knew who had done it. Flames shot up probably higher than the movie's roof-top. People screamed and began to panic, followed by Bozan running back and forth screaming "police, fire, police, fire." The crowd retreated and collided with the throng that had entered the theater and who were desperately looking for seats.

The three of us, doubled up with laughter, laughter fueled by panicky sweaty Bozan, the frightened crowd, and the flames in front of the door. I will never know how things calmed down on their own nor , how we were not yet to fired(eventually we were fired disgracefully). Bozan would never have believed it even if we were to have confessed.

Later on, Harry and Anthony filled in the details. They had gathered as many of the discarded Christmas trees that they could find and piled them up outside of the movie doors. Having synchronized their watches ,they knew to the second as to when I would open the doors. The trees were lit and an immediate bonfire began.

It was at about this age(18) that the four compadres and a host of others entered the world of motorcycles. Now, our reign of terror spread out over a larger part of the city and the Yorkville map.

**Marc and Roger in the front, Harry to the right,
Artie all the way back**

CHAPTER **15**

Coney Island

CONEY ISLAND, THAT Brooklyn landmark which still exists in diminished form today, was visited by millions during the Summer season. The wooden boardwalk that spread out over the beach and thousands of umbrellas below, stretched on for what seemed forever.

Young and old, families and lovers, and sunbathers dotted the horizon next to the water's edge. They would spend all day there from morning until sunset baking like lobsters.

All day long, the boardwalk buzzed with activity. Landmarks such as Nathan's offered foot long frankfurters, sodas, and the best French fries and potato knishes that could be found anywhere.

Every inch of the boardwalk was taken by concession stands and all kinds of penny arcades that featured games from penny slot machines to more expensive ones that yielded all kinds of prizes.

Carnival rides and restaurants adorned the boardwalk and the adjoining side streets. There were rides like the parachute, roller coaster, the barrel , and many more. The barrel was interesting as it was a gigantic barrel into which a person entered and tried to stand without falling as it revolved at faster accelerating speeds.

There were side shows which were supposed to contain odd creatures and monsters. A human barker would aggressively attempt to get you to purchase a ticket for this show. Armed with large megaphones, these side show salesmen were good at their craft. Once inside, we were greeted by dimly lit rooms which housed not monsters or odd people but, people with illnesses that were manifested through grotesque bodies that bore the stamp of their particular disease.

Coney Island
Public domain picture from the Internet

Another great attraction was the Steeplechase. For a fixed price, you could get tickets for a wide variety of rides and entertainment. Everything from clowns who whacked peoples'

buttocks with large paddles and with air pumps that would blow up a woman's dress before anticipating audiences, were a mainstay here.

These clowns waited for those exiting the rides inside. An already initiated audience sat or stood and shouted with glee as the clowns administered their mischief. Women wearing dresses were the unlucky ones as the air pumps blew their dresses so that a full view of their undergarments was common. Now and again, an unwitting participant , scantily dressed, brought down the duck(On an old T.V. show, The Groucho Marx program, if the word of the day were uttered by a contestant, a toy duck would come down from the ceiling).It was all in good fun as everyone took the clowns' antics rather well.

After eating until swollen, the long exodus homeward began. This probably was the farthest away from our home turf, Yorkville, that as kids we ever were.

Our mothers were great sports to bring us there, spend the whole day, and then take us back.

Going and coming, the trains were our means of transportation. They were overcrowded and hot and filled to capacity with exhausted people. If one were lucky, he could get a seat. The less fortunate had to stand and grab the straps that hung from long bars or just lean against another unfortunate soul like bookends.

I remember the chafing of my skin from a tightfitting bathing suit saturated with ocean salt and beach sand. Once home, we had to climb five flights of stairs to enter a sweltering apartment.

CHAPTER 16

John Jay Park

JOHN JAY PARK , located on East 77th street next to the F.D.R. drive and the East River, had a public swimming pool which was always well attended.

For ten cents, we could stay there for either the morning session until noon or from 1 P.M. until closing at 6P.M. Everyone from the neighborhood showed up and lines were long. After paying the ten cents, we could use the lockers and showers located inside. We had to shower before entering the pool.

There was a large tarlike softball "field" next to the swimming pool and adjacent to the "field" were four handball courts. Along the sides of these were benches where families sat while their children played games. We also had Carl Schurtz and Central Park in our backyards.

It was a hot summer's night and Peter_____and I walked down to John Jay park to see what we could cook up. Although Peter was not one of the steadfast little bastards, he would hang with us from time to time.

I believe that it was in fifth grade when the following incident occurred. Peter and I were standing against the rail fence that enclosed the park from the highway below. Between the park and the highway was a narrow street where people walked their dogs or hung out and drank. On this particularly warm spring evening, we stood against the fence (each bar had spaces of about 10 inches between them) and we noticed a man walking his dog just below us. He stopped for some time and Peter began to urinate on his head. I remember that he was bald, perhaps of middle age, and his dog was not too large.

As the urine splashed on his head, it sprayed in different directions. He did not look up until Peter finished what he was doing. I simultaneously began to laugh and tremble with fear. I knew that our chances of receiving a beating at the hands of this man were good. The man looked up and began to dry his head with a handkerchief and calmly asked, " Hey kid, is that water ?"Peter shouted, "It's piss." The man screamed out a long line of curses and let his dog go. He began to run around the park in an attempt to get us. We started to run and knew that it would be close. The entrance and exit were one and there was only one way out.

As we approached the exit, the man's dog was close by with the man right behind him. By some miracle, we beat him to the exit and continued running. He kept on the chase for another block and gave up. I was grateful to have escaped with my life but I laughed anyway.

CHAPTER 17

Motorcycle Days

OUR MOTORCYCLE DAYS had their beginning with Rogers' father Angelo who would announce his arrival home from his three shifts with the "put, put" of his Vespa motorscooter. It was a small machine with a small wheel base but it was the catalyst of our motorcycle activities. Of course, Roger soon "inherited" the Vespa and the seeds of our motorcycle activities were planted. I immediately went out and spent all of my savings from the after school jobs and bought one to be soon followed by Harry and Marc. I couldn't wait to ride and being unlicensed, I began to break the law and was on the road. Roger, who was good with his hands, fashioned a fake license plate out of cardboard, crayons, and paint. The plate flew up and down when the wind blew adding to the risk that we were taking.

Eventually we passed the road test and convinced Happy and Marc to part with their savings and buy a machine. In time Harry worked his way up to a Harley Davidson 74 (the Hog) and Marc, to a B.S.A.

Cars were out of our reach and so we rode our motorcycles day and night year round in all kind of weather. I eventually tired of the limited capability of the Vespa and graduated up to a Honda "Superhawk" 305ccs , The same bike that the actor Paul Newman used to race.

The antics that we perpetrated without wheels now were duplicated on our bikes. As the group grew in numbers with the addition of the "Lords" motorcycle gang which included Peter G., Mad Dog Green, Neal___- and other fringe members, we would meet on 81st Street and there we would start our bikes simultaneously with the revving of the engine reaching a deafening pitch. Soon the tenement dwellers would look out their windows and start screaming at us from the safety of their apartments. Once we felt we aggravated them enough we would head out to other neighborhoods in search of who knows what. Black leather jackets and jeans were our uniform. Girls who rode in back wore the same. No one sported helmets as the law requiring the wearing of helmets was not in existence in 1966.

Harry seemed to be the group's leader because he had the Harley Davidson 74. The other bikes included Yamahas, Hondas, Bultacos, BMWs, and Kawasakis.

One of our most harmless pranks, and Harry's idea, was to go to the annual New York City Easter Parade which ran on Fifth Avenue , with our bikes. We put on bizarre costumes and with mischief in our hearts , headed for the parade.

Harry led the pack with his Harley and our entering the parade was surprisingly easy. We knew that the parade was only for pedestrians and that added to the excitement. Of course we were stopped by a policeman who angrily demanded an explanation as to what we were doing in the parade with our bikes.

Having signaled us to a complete halt, the policeman told Harry to pull over and at which point, Harry pulled a beauty.

"There's a flower in my engine " Harry said . The cop quite baffled by all of this asked, "What flower?" Harry repeated the flower bit and the policeman was totally confused. I laughed surreptitiously as the officer was reaching his boiling point. "What flower?" he demanded. Harry pointed to his engine and invited the officer to see for himself. The officer went down on all fours and began looking for the phantom flower. As he searched in vain, Harry gunned the engine. We all took off and rode the bikes onto the sidewalk where throngs of pedestrians were strolling. Curses and clenched fists aimed in our direction from the strollers added more spice to the occasion.

To this day, I don't know how we were able to ride away from the angry and probably embarrassed policeman and get away with riding on the parade's sidewalk.

One of our more memorable "actions" was performed on the F.D.R. Drive which runs from125th Street and the East River down past Houston Street and around the West Side of Manhattan. We would drive two abreast in one lane with a passenger on the back of the cycle. Filling the three lanes with two machines in each lane gave a line of six cycles in a row going 50 to 60 MPH. Cars stuck behind this line of cycles could not pass. At a given signal, the driver would stand up and hold his arms out like a cross as the cycle piloted itself. Cars coming from the opposite lanes of the highway gaped in surprise as we led the parade of cars that were tailing us.

Neil____, while driving on his own was known to pop a "wheely" (where the cycle rides on the back tire only at a 45 degree angle while traveling at high speed). This was risky to say the least.

Our ventures on bikes included a trip to Bear Mountain and speeding at 85MPH banking our bikes around the many curves in the road. The girls on the back loved these excursions and in these large groups, we were like Marlon Brando in the film "The Wild Ones" or so we thought.

Bear Mountain Ride

Like in a movie script, on one warm summer evening twenty bikes made their way down the Belt Parkway and wound up in Staten Island. We stopped at a diner and as we pulled up, the panic stricken proprietor pulled down the window blinds and hung a "closed" sign on the door. We contemplated retaliating but decided to move on.

The four , no longer little bastards, would get together almost every day and plan trouble of one kind or another on their cycles. One such activity included driving on the side walk and chasing pedestrians into the gutter. Curses and clenched fists followed us wherever we went.

When girls rode on the back of the cycles, our behavior became almost normal. Needless to say, the girls were treated with the greatest respect. Even we had some standards.

We all started out together in elementary school and came to the point of riding motorcycles together for a few years. All aspects of life revolved around our love of riding and together we rode on to college (surprisingly not jail).

CCNY was then as it is now a very liberal college . The Lords thought it would be a nice gesture to break up a disruptive anti -Vietnam demonstration which was being held on campus. Machines met the bones of protesters who scattered like frightened hens. This act, and others like it, such as taking over the cafeteria earned us a front page article in the college's campus newspaper, The Campus. Our infamy on campus grew and we were given a wide berth wherever we went on the school grounds.

It was during my senior year at CCNY that the end came for me. I was driving down Convent Avenue at City College between the change of classes making a one half mile trip quickly from the North Campus to the South Campus. Hitting 50MPH on this narrow two way street I saw a large car attempting to turn from Convent Avenue into a small side street. The car pulled right in front of me. I hit the brakes and headed right for the slow turning car. In my mind I said "This is it!" as I slammed into the side of the car. On impact I flew into the air and witnesses related that I somersaulted twice before landing on the roof of the car on my back. Stunned, wearing my leather jacket and a beret, I shook my head, jumped off the roof of the car and saw my beautiful bike crushed like an accordion. When the police arrived, I shakily informed them to take my bike away and, as in a dream, I walked away.

It must have been divine retribution for all of my deeds that I came so close to being dead on "Convent" Avenue.

Some of us are gone now and others have moved away, or are leading lives of denial of the past.

We had good times on the bikes, there was trouble, and sometimes the police were involved, but, at the end of the day, the original little bastards were just that, little bastards.

Marc

Roger

Artie and Marc

Marc and Harry

The Lords Motorcycle Club

Last Thoughts

I SINCERELY HOPE that those of you who had the patience and interest in reading this memoir, did find that it sparked a memory or two, and even a laugh or a tear as it did me.

These memories are just that, memories. The incidents and characters will never return and someone has to keep it alive.

There are many books about the history of Yorkville which are important but don't have the inner wrinkle on the people that lived there. Although, not of importance to scholars, these people formed the fabric of our most interesting neighborhood. How lucky I was to have so much yet own so little. We had the most unique growing experience that one could imagine.

I thank you old timers and young people that took the time to read about our lives in memory lane.

The Neighborhood

PS158

The library on East 78th Street

The stoop on East 81st Street